Zen Wisdom

Zen Wisdom
The Way to the Top

Editors:
Ashikaga Yoshiharu and Rosemary Brant

Astrolog Publishing House Ltd

Cover Design: Na'ama Yaffe

P. O. Box 1123, Hod Hasharon 45111, Israel
Tel: 972-9-7412044
Fax: 972-9-7442714

ISBN 965-494-213-5

Published by
Astrolog Publishing House 2006

INTRODUCTION

Zen Wisdom is a collection of theories of Chinese Zen adepts from the Song dynasty, from the tenth to the thirteenth century. One may call the Tang dynasty (seventh to ninth centuries) the "classical era" of Zen. While the Zen literature of the Tang dynasty is simple and direct, the literature of the Song dynasty is artistic and complex.

Zen experts of the Song era noticed at the time the spread of many artificial kinds of Zen, imitations of ways to realize Zen. The popularity of artificial Zen was intensified due to the great impact that the original Zen had had on the Asian culture.

This book, *Zen Wisdom*, contains many significant notes concerning the downfall of the superiority of the institutions of Zen and its believers.

In the history of Eastern Asia, Zen had a singular role in the artificial restoration and renewal of the original spiritual science of Buddhism by creating schools for religion, philosophy, literature, art, music, psychology, psychiatry, social studies, and physical education.

Zen Wisdom illustrates the art of purifying the final truth – day-to-day as well as eternal – while using society and its conduct to attain Zen enlightenment by implementing constructive criticism and higher education.

The classical era of Chinese Zen is usually classed as belonging to the Tang dynasty, from the seventh until the ninth century. During the Tang era, Zen revolutionized the habits of society that lasted for centuries. Zen offered one of the sole platforms in history for unbiased social comprehension, as well as spiritual comprehension.

Zen also influenced two of the most important areas of Chinese art – painting and poetry. These two areas were traditionally used for spiritual education and therefore held great social significance.

During the Song era, institutions aimed to release humankind from the poison of greed, violence and ignorance that prevented humanity from reaching the full practical comprehension of its real goal.

Recognizing Zen is what's called in popular language "enlightenment". In Zen, enlightenment is considered to be the preface to higher educational experiences available to humankind.

With the decline of the Song era, there was already a significant standard in the design of many aspects of the process of Zen, demanded by a growing number of followers who streamed to the gates of the glorified institutions of Zen. At the time, the discipline of the public monasteries evolved under governmental supervision where renowned Zen masters were invited to teach large assemblies, during summer and winter study periods.

In the original Zen communities everyone had to work, and duties were assigned according to one's abilities as perceived by the handful of experts who guided the community.

The origins of most of the famous literature of the Song dynasty, which is in fact the classical literature of Zen, derive from the public lessons of its teachers. As a result, it's very vague and veiled as appropriate to the secretive nature of the Zen experience.

Contrary to that, these *Zen Wisdom* is based on personal guidance and private teaching and as a result, are much more obvious.

See also *Zen Teachings*, ISBN 9654942054, 2005.

Notes on Sources

In original Chinese *Zen Wisdom* (and *Zen Teachings*) are called *Chanlin baoxun*, or *Chanmen Baoxun*, "Precious Lessons from the Chan (Zen) Schools".

They were originally assembled in the early twelfth century by two extraordinary Zen masters, Miaoxi (better known as Dahui) and Zhu-an. At the end of the twelfth century, this collection was further extended by Zen master Jingshan, to the textual form existing today. During the next five hundred years, a number of notes that appear in the text were written in China. The book was first published in Japan in 1279, one hundred years after its recompilation.

Zen Wisdom illustrates the personal studies of the Zen masters of the early Song dynasty. Much of the material is taken from unusual sources that are difficult to obtain or that no longer exist. It was therefore possible to obtain this material in its original only through direct contact with the network of Zen schools. Several selections from the assortment aren't ascribed to any written source and it's possible that they were written by one or the other of the compilers who relied on the material derived from the oral tradition of the time. Zen Lessons provides us rare glimpses of distinguished masters and preserves a large part of the unique Zen wisdom that would have otherwise been lost to later generations.

Zen Wisdom is an exclusive part of the huge body of the Chan Buddhism theory from the Song dynasty that still exists in written form. This text clarifies that Chan Buddhism literature was considerably more comprehensive than the large collection of current Chan writings.

Countless anthologies are quoted in *Zen Wisdom*; most of these collections no longer exist, not including the unusual occurrence of the huge collection of the Tanqin Annals. Apparently, all that's left of them is what we find in *Zen Wisdom*. These sources are sometimes given abbreviated titles and at times are referred to only by common names.

Other sources include diaries, engraved inscriptions and letters. They contain rare reports concerning famous masters, especially selected by the original compilers due to the fact that they weren't written in cipher and because of their implementation in social matters.

ZEN WISDOM

RULES

"The general design of the original rules of Chan communities was to show what was right, rein in what is wrong, provide a model and introduce equality to the community, and through this, control the feelings of the future generations according to the times.

Human feelings are like water, rules and manners are like a dam. If the dam isn't strong enough, water will burst through it. If human feelings are not controlled, they will be spoiled and wild. Therefore, in order to get rid of feelings and stop illusions, in order to prevent evil and put an end to mistakes, we mustn't forget the guiding rules for a moment.

But how can rules and manners completely oppress human feelings? They too, are steps that help a person enter the Way.

Establishing rules is as clear as the sun and moon – those who act by them can't get lost; they are as wide as a highway – those who travel on it can't get confused. The ancient sages were organized differently, but when you go back to the source you find no difference.

Among Chan communities of today, there are those who vigorously act according to regulations, there are those who stick to the regulations until the bitter end, there are those who scorn the regulations – all of them have strayed from the Way and lost the principle. The cause of this is indulgence and adherence to the wrong things.

These people never consider the ancient sages who saved the next generation from degeneration and prevented a slack and lenient atmosphere by putting a stop to their indulgent state of mind, cutting off the path of errors and prejudice. That is the reason for the organization."

BALANCE

"Students must engrave on their hearts truthfulness and balance. Then, even if they are tripped in a hundred ways, they will stay calm and unconcerned.

But if they have inclinations or prejudice, and they waste days and nights on the petty effort of gaining a profit, I fear there is no place between heaven and earth for their enormous body."

THE LEGACY OF EXTRAVAGANCE

"When Gaoan heard that life was extravagant at Jinshan while Cheng Gumu was the leader there, he felt a deep sadness, and said, 'The value of restriction does not burden decency – how can something like this be considered correct? How can someone, for no reason, leave luxurious habits to the future generations, while increasing insatiable demands and feel no shame from the ancients?'"

Slogans

"Students mustn't get stuck on words and sayings. In general, relying on the sayings of others in order to phrase your comprehension, blocks the way to your own enlightenment, and you cannot make progress beyond literal symbols. In ancient times, when Da Guanpi first saw Master Shimen Cong in private discussions, he practiced his eloquence. But Shimen said to him, 'What you say are words on a paper – you haven't entered the necessary subtlety of your complex mind. You must strive for indescribable enlightenment; when enlightened you will rise far and above, you will not ride on words or stick to phrases and you will be like the roaring lion who all the other beasts fear. Then, when you look back on the study of words, it will be like comparing ten and a hundred, like comparing a thousand to a multitude.'"

THE STATE OF THE COMMUNITY

"The community is a house to the great body of the leader. Distinctions are given accordingly; expenses are suited to the vessel, the activity considers the principles of peace and well-being, gain and loss stem from the source of the teachings. How can it be easy to serve as a model for people?

I've never seen a negligent and relaxed leader win the obedience of his flock, nor one who abandoned his rules and goals to prevent the Chan community from becoming despicable savages. In ancient times, Master Yuwang Shen fired his senior student, and Master Yangshan Wei expelled his attendant. These cases are listed in our writings and should be taken as standards. These days, everyone follows his own personal indulgence, thus ruining the basic principles of the Chan community to a great measure.

People these days, are lazy about getting up, and most of them lack manners when they assemble. There are those who shamelessly indulge in gluttony, others create fights while pushing forward to obtain gain and honor. Things have reached a point when there is no longer a place where you won't find the ugliness of opportunism.

How can we ever succeed in the ways of truth and have the full power for the spiritual study that we search for?"

HABIT

"Enlightenment, humanity and righteousness are not the lot of ancients only; people of our time have them as well, but because their knowledge isn't clear, their studies narrow, their abilities impure and their will weak, they cannot carry them out with power. Finally, they are diverted by what they see and hear, which causes them to be unaware of their situation.

Everything is due to misleading conceptions and emotional thinking, which accumulate into a pile of habit that can't be eliminated all at once. This is the only reason why people of these times don't reach the ranks of the ancients."

WHAT ARE YOU DOING?

"It is told, that while Gaoan was the leader of the Yunju community, he would scold students who failed to seriously comprehend his private teaching methods, saying, 'Your parents nourished your body, your teachers and friends formed your mind. You are not oppressed because of cold and hunger; you don't have to work hard in military service. Under these conditions, if you don't make a dedicated effort to correctly practice the Way, how can you face your parents, teachers, and friends?'

Some students cried when they heard the words of their enlightened teacher.

Such was his order – fair and strict."

16

THE HOUSE OF THE RETIRED

"When Gaoan retired from the leadership of Yunju, Master Yuanwu wanted to repair the Reclining Dragon Hermitage that Foyan had built and make it into a place of rest for Gaoan.

Gaoan said, 'If the forest-man has true joy in his heart, he can ignore the body. I am seventy years old, and am like the morning star or the moon – how much more time have I left? In the Lu hills of the western mountains, a place where the rocky forests and streams adjoin, they are all suitable places for me to retire in my old age – why do I need a place for myself before I can enjoy it?'

After a short time, he took his people and went to holy Mount Tiantai and later died on Flower Peak."

THE INFLUENCE OF CONDUCT

"When Gaoan was the leader of the Yunju community, he would lament and grieve every time he heard of a student who fell ill and had been moved to the revivification hall, as if he himself had fallen ill. Day and night he asked about their health, and would personally concoct medicines and boil porridge for them, which he gave them only after he first tasted it himself. If the weather was cold, he would rub their backs and say, 'Do you have enough clothes on?' When it was hot, he would gaze into their faces and ask them if they were too warm.

If unfortunately, someone fell ill and it was impossible to save him, Gaoan would not ask what the student did or didn't have, but would carry out all the funeral procedures according to what was available in the treasury.

Once, when one of the monastery officers refused to make such an expenditure, Gaoan scolded him, saying:

'In ancient times, the founders of Chan communities established the treasury for the sake of the weak and old. You are not ill and not dead.'

Perceptive people from all around greatly appreciated Gaoan's personal conduct. When he retired from Yunju and went to Mount Tiantai, fifty students followed him. Those who couldn't join him, wept as he parted from them. This is how much his virtue touched people."

EDUCATION

"There are no wise or foolish students. It all depends on the teacher's ability to refine them in order to bring out the virtuous actions within them, examine them in order to discover their hidden abilities, stimulate and encourage them, give weight to their words, take care that they complete their practice. In the many months and long years to come, their name and surrounding reality will both grow rich.

The spirit lies within all people – it is all just a matter of careful guidance. It is just like a precious stone embedded in a rock – if you throw it away, it is a rock, but if you cut it and polish it, it is a precious stone. The same with water sprouting from a spring, block it and it becomes a swamp, dig a deep canal for it, and it becomes a river.

And so we know that even in these times of imitation of teachings and remnants of teachings it isn't intelligence that is lost or unused, there is also something lacking in the way young people are educated and raised.

When the Chan communities flourished fully, the people in those communities were the leftovers of the last generation of Buddhism. Those left corrupt were the fools while those who took responsibility for their personal development were the wise. This is why I say that everyone has the spirit, but it needs strict guidance.

Therefore, we recognize our students' abilities, and the ups and downs of times on which they can rely if properly treated – excel if encouraged; decline if oppressed, and perish if denied. This is the basis of debauchery or development of the virtues and abilities of the students."

THE GREATNESS OF TEACHING

"There is nothing more important for the greatness of teaching than virtue and decency. When a leader respects decency, his students will value reverence and respect. When the leader acts properly, the students are ashamed to be greedy and competitive.

If the leader is sloppy and shameful, his students will become contemptuous hooligans – an obstacle unto themselves.

If the leader gets into disputes and loses his temper, his students will be quick-tempered and argumentative – a calamity unto themselves.

Ancient sages had a prior knowledge that brought them to choose enlightened knights of wisdom to lead the Chan community, thereby causing the people who observed them to change of their own accord.

That is why when the studies of the Way flourished thanks to the great ancient adepts, extraordinary people appeared. Their conduct was gentle and noble, harmonious, peaceful, and tidy.

This is how they should be, those whose every word and action could be guides for future generations."

NOTHING TO BE ASHAMED OF

"Gaoan was a strong and upright person from within and without. His character was strict and his conduct was always proper. When he was a student, he was attacked and slandered again and again, but he never paid too much attention. All his life he carried himself with simplicity and modesty.

In private teachings he never expressed an irresponsible opinion. If there was any sort of dispute, he would handle it severely, in direct terms. All the students believed in him and accepted his teaching.

Once he said, 'My teaching of the Way is not greater than others. It is just that I have never done a thing that I have to be ashamed of in my heart.'"

BEYOND THE RANGE OF MONKS

"When Gaoan was abbot of the Yunju monastery, when he saw monks attacking others for their hidden faults, he would scold them with these words, 'The fact is not this. For people in a monastery, the Way alone – along with self-development – is an urgent and immediate matter. How can you indulge yourselves with likes and dislikes while slandering other peoples actions?' So cautious and considerate he was.

At first, Master Gaoan wouldn't accept the abbacy in Yunju monastery, but the elder master Foyan sent him a letter that urged him to take the leadership of the monastery. The letter read, 'Yunju is a leading monastery in the region; there you can settle the community and continue with the Way. You shouldn't persist on refusing.'

Gaoan said, 'Ever since there have been monasteries, there have been many students who have had their principles ruined because of this name.'

When the elder master Fojian heard this, he said, 'Gaoan's conduct is beyond the range of monks.'"

A MAN OF PERCEPTION

"When Gaoan addressed an assembly he would always say, 'When in a group, one should always know when there is a man of perception.' I asked him what he meant and Gaoan answered, 'Haven't you read the words of Guishan, 'In your actions, take an example from the superiors, don't follow the vulgar and mediocre'? These are the words of those who, despite their daily interference with the crowd, didn't sink into low foolishness.'

Among the mass, many are vulgar; few are "knowers". It is easy to get used to the vulgar, hard to get close to the "knowers".

If you can develop your will so that you are comparable to one man facing a thousand enemies until the power of vulgarity passes from the world, then you will truly be supreme, beyond measure."

SIGNS OF GOOD LEADERSHIP

"When Master Xuetang led the Qianfu community, he one day asked one of the new students where he had come from. The student said that he had come from Fujian. Xuetang said, 'Did you see any good leaders along the way?'

The student said, 'Lately I passed through this and this region and although I have never met Master Ben of Poshan, I know he is supposed to be a good leader.'

Xuetang said, 'How do you know that he's good?'

The monk said, 'When you enter that monastery, the paths there are clear, the halls are in good shape, lights and incense are always burning in the shrines, the sounds of bells and drums are sounded accurately and clearly every evening and morning, the food is good and clean, and the monks are polite. This is how I know that Ben is a good leader.'

Xuetang smiled and said, 'It is obvious that Ben is wise and that you have eyes in your head.' He then reported these words to the governor of the county and added, 'I am getting old and I am asking you to invite Ben and ask him to be the leader at Qianfu, in hope that the work of the Chan community prospers.'"

INWARD CONTROL, OUTWARD VIRTUE

"When I was young I heard these words from my father, 'Without inward control a person cannot stand, and without outward virtue a person cannot act.' This saying is worth practicing all your life; embodied in it is the work of sages and saints.

I remembered these words and cultivated myself while living at home. Even now, when I am the leader of a group, these words are like a balance stone weighing the light and heavy, like a compass and rule defining round and square. Without it there would be chaos."

SINISTER DESTRUCTION

"An iron dam a thousand miles long leaks through anthills. The beauty of a precious stone is lost as a result of hidden flaws. The mysteriously supreme Way is way beyond iron dams and precious stones, and yet greed and anger are stronger than anthills and flaws.

The essence of the matter is in true and clear desire, in actions that become progressively refined, in firm and sure industriousness, the cultivation being completely purified. After that, it is possible to benefit oneself and others."

IRON FACE BING

"When I was the leader of the community at Longmen, Iron Face Bing was the leader of the community at Taiping. Someone told me that when Bing first went on study travels, before he had left his native home for long, he suddenly took his teacher's notes and burned them in the fire. At the time, whenever he received a letter, he would throw it to the ground and say that it was just a waste of time."

ENERGY AND WILL

"When the energy of students is stronger than their will, they become small, petty people. When their will controls their energy, they become true, upright people. When their will and energy are equal, they become enlightened sages.

There are people who are stubbornly hostile and won't see a warning in any guidance – it is their energy that makes them like that. True and upright people, even if they are forced to do something wrong, will stay steady and agreeable till their end – it is their will that makes them like this."

REFLECTIONS

"While managing affairs, one must consider the light and heavy issues; when publicly speaking one must first think and reflect. Strive for the middle way; don't allow deviations.

Rash and careless actions rarely bring success. Even if it is possible to succeed this way, it eventually ends badly.

When I was in a community of students, I experienced loss and gain fully. Only those of virtue moved people by their generosity. I hope that in the future, those who have will-power will practice this responsibly. That in itself will be a supreme achievement.

Lingyuan used to say, 'Usually, when people are immersed in inner reflections, they can understand much in a clear fashion, but when involved in matters occurring outside, they will oppose the integration and lose touch with reality.'

If you truly think of inheriting the responsibility of the enlightened teachers, I direct you to examine and criticize yourself all the time."

CLAD IN A PATCHWORK ROBE

"It is told that when Master Yingan Hua was the exemplar of the community of Miaoguo monastery, the elder master Xuetang used to visit him every day.

There were some who criticized Xuetang for this, but his answer was, 'My spiritual nephew Hua doesn't delight in gain or strive for fame. He doesn't prefer praises to criticism, he isn't pleasant or conciliatory for gain, he doesn't wear false masks or use clever words. Add that to the fact that he sees the Way in perfect clarity, and can stop or proceed as he wishes, and you have a person clad in a patchwork robe such as is hard to find. Therefore, I respect him."

PERSECUTION

"When Lingyuan was the leader of the Chan community in Taiping, he was unjustly persecuted by certain government officials. Lingyuan wrote a letter to our late teacher Wuzu, 'It is getting to be impossible to carry out the Way straight ahead, and it isn't my wish to be leader by being crooked. I prefer a free mind among thousands of cliffs and countless ravines, living daily on straw and millet for the rest of my life. Why bother anymore?'

Not ten days had passed, and Lingyuan was requested to lead the community at Huanglong. He grasped the opportunity and left."

HUMAN FIGURES

"Lingyuan liked classifying paupers by comparisons. He quoted an ancient saying, 'It is like creating human figures from clay and wood. When one carves a figure from wood, the nose and ears must be big at first, while the mouth and eyes must be small so that if the artist gets them wrong, the nose and ears will be made smaller, while the mouth and eyes can be made bigger.

'When making a human figure from clay, the ears and nose must be made small at first, and the eyes and mouth big at first. If the artist gets them wrong, the nose and ears can be made bigger, while the mouth and eyes can be made smaller.'

Even though this saying might seem insignificant, it can be used as an allegory of the great. If students have to make a choice before an event, do not tire of 'thinking it over three times,' they may be called after that sincere people."

A LIFE OF FREEDOM

"Wanan accompanied Gaoan to the holy Mount Tiantai. When they returned, Wanan told me that the elder Deguan lived there, secluded among the crags for thirty years, during which time he hadn't left the mountain. Mr. Long Xuetan, the district magistrate and a follower of Chan Buddhism, offered an invitation to Deguan to become abbot of the Ruiyan monastery, but Deguan refused with a poem:

> *For thirty years of solitary I've closed the door,*
> *How can this vocation reach the green mountain?*
> *Stop trying to use the trivialities of the human world*
> *To exchange for my life of freedom in the forest.*

The invitation was sent again, but in the end, Deguan never went to the monastery. Mr. Long admired him and compared him to Yinshan, one of the greatest ancient monks.

And Wanan also said there was an old man there that remembered Deguan's words, 'Failing to comprehend the Way, enthusiasm with material objects, confusing thoughts with feelings, having the heart of a wolf and the mind of a fox, flattery and deceit, bowing one's head to authorities, agreeing in order to be liked, pursuing fame and profit, turning away from what is real and running after what is false, turning one's back on enlightenment and joining the dust of the earth – forest people of the Way do not act like this."

Rich and Noble

"Xuetang was born in a rich and noble home, but he had no habits of boastfulness and lavishness. He stayed modest and frugal, was pure and unconcerned with material things.

Once someone gave him as a present an iron mirror, but Xuetang gave it away and said, 'The spring in the valley is clear enough to reflect even hair or whiskers – what need have I for this mirror?'"

LEARNERS AND AMATEURS

"Xuetang was humane and merciful, honest and compassionate. He admired the wise and respected the talented. Jokes and trivialities almost never left his mouth. He wasn't cold or unapproachable, and never acted harshly or in anger. In his actions he was steady and pure.

Once he said, 'When the ancients studied the Way, they were indifferent to outside influences and erased natural desires, until they reached a point where they completely forgot about authority and rank, and left the world of form and sound. They seemed to have abilities without studying. Students now use all their wisdom, but in the end they are helpless. Why is this? If the will isn't steady, and the task isn't focused, you will just be an amateur.'"

YOURSELF AND OTHERS

"Yuantong Xiu once said, 'If a person cannot be upright, and yet requests others to be so, that is called a lapse of virtue. If he isn't respectful but asks others to be, that is called a violation of decency.

If a person who serves as a teacher lapses from virtue and goes against decency, what can be used to extend the future guidelines?'"

Not in the Forefront

"If you wish to seek the great spiritual Way, first set right your mind. If you have any anger in you, you cannot set right your mind. And if you have any desires you won't be able to set right your mind. Anyway, who besides saints and sages is free from like and dislike, happiness and anger?

Therefore, all you have to do is not give these issues first preference lest they harm rectitude. That itself is considered an achievement."

THE FASTEST SHORTCUT

"In order to enter the Way, the fastest shortcut is based on moderation and concession. I see many students with enthusiastic minds and stuttering mouths, eager to succeed the ancient Chans, but when I search for moderation and concession, I can't find one in ten thousand.

These are like sons of a family who want to be officials, but aren't willing to make the effort to read a book. Even a little Confucian boy knows that this isn't possible."

DECENCY AND TRUSTWORTHINESS

"Decency and trustworthiness are essential in word and action to the craft of leadership. When your words are decent and trustworthy, the impression they make is deep; when they are not, the impression they make is shallow.

There is no place, even in the ordinary life of this world, for indecent words and untrustworthy actions, for fear that one be slighted by people. And even more so when one is acting as the leader of a community, spreading the teaching of virtue and enlightenment. If you lack decency and trustworthiness in your words and actions, who in the world will follow you?"

NATURE

"My late teacher Huitang said, 'Openness and generosity were given to people by nature – when you try to force them, they won't last long. A person who acts forcefully, but who isn't enduring, will receive scorn and mockery from petty people.' In the same way, true and false, good and bad, are given by nature as well, and cannot be changed.

Only people with a balanced nature, who can deal with great and small, are worth relating with and teaching."

THE WAY AND MATERIALISM

"Seeking profit has nothing in common with the Way, seeking the Way has no connection with profit. It isn't because the ancients couldn't unite them, but because their forces do not accord.

If the Way and profit-seeking would walk together, what need would the ancients have to give up their status and wealth, forget achievements and fame, torment their minds and bodies in empty mountains and wide swamps, and live off spring water and fruit for the rest of their lives?

If you insist on saying that profit-making and the Way could be materialized without any mutual interference, it as if you said to pour wine from a leaking cup onto a burning pot – there is no way you can save it this way."

IMPARTIALITY

"There is a story about when Master Sixin was leader of the community at the Cuiyan monastery, he heard that Master Jiaofan had been banished from the continent. On his way to his place of exile on the southern island of Hainan, he passed through the region of Cuiyan. Sixin sent a group to meet Jiaoan and bring him back to the monastery where he generously took care of him for several days and then sorrowfully saw him off. Some people who noticed that Sixin had criticized Jiaoan in the past, claimed that Sixin was fickle.

Sixin said, 'Jiaoan is a virtuous wearer of a patchwork robe. I used extreme words in the past in order to remove the brazenness of his superiority. Now that he has become entangled in foul play, this is his lot. I acted according to the usual principles of Chan communities.'

Those who know, say that Sixin acted this way because he had no partiality regarding people."

FEELINGS

"The tire that burns the field starts from a small flame, the river that wears away a mountain starts from one drop. A pile of dust can block a little flow of water, but when the flow is powerful it can uproot trees, dislodge boulders and erase hills. A spark of fire can be extinguished with a glass of water, but a great flame can burn down cities, villages and forests.

Is this different from the water of affection and closeness, or the fire of anger and malice?

When ancient people controlled their minds, they stopped their thoughts before they arose, stopped their feelings before they awoke. Therefore, they used very little energy while the achievements they obtained were so much greater. When feeling and nature are at odds, and love and hate mix and conflict, then in one person it harms one's life and in his relations with others it will harm their beings. How great the danger is, beyond salvation."

CONTROLLING PREJUDICE

"There is nothing special about leadership – basically it deals with   controlling the evils of biased information and tyranny.

Do not act rashly on the basis of what is said first – then the trivialities of petty people will not able to confuse you.

After all, the feelings of a group aren't one, and it's difficult to see common sense. You must examine something in order to see if it withholds benefit or harm, examine whether or not it is appropriate and fitting; after that you may act."

DISCERNING FEELINGS

"There is nothing as important in leadership than a responsible observation of people's situation and knowing them all, the upper and lower class.

When the mental conditions of people are fully understood, then inside and outside are in harmony. When above and below connect, everything is done suitably. This way leadership is secure.

If the leader cannot minutely discern people's mental conditions, and the feelings of the people below aren't communicated above, then things go wrong, above and below contradict each other. This is how leadership is ruined.

It may happen that a leader will rely on his brilliant mind, which frequently carries prejudice, failing to comprehend people's feelings, rejecting the advice of his community and give too much importance to his own authority while neglecting public considerations and preferring private favoritism. This causes the road of progress towards goodness to grow narrower and narrower, and the path of communal responsibility to become fainter and fainter.

These leaders avoid anything they haven't seen or heard in the past and are stuck with patterns of behavior to which they are used to and by which they are veiled.

To hope that the leadership of these people be great and of great influence is like walking backwards when trying to go forward."

Natural Selection

"My late teacher Huitang said, 'In a large community, the virtuous and the corrupt live together, because of the greatness of the teaching. And so, one can't help but be drawn to some of the people and avoid the company of others. It is possible to select a little more subtly.'

One mustn't estrange oneself because of personal resentment from people with abilities and virtues who meet with the expectations of the community. And if there are people with ordinary traits who are disliked by the community, you mustn't befriend them because of personal liking. If you act this way, then the virtuous will advance on their own, the corrupt will regress on their own, and the community is at peace.

If the leader indulges in personal feelings and appoints or demotes people as a result of personal liking or resentment, he causes the virtuous to stay contained and silent while the corrupt compete for the high positions. The structure of the institutions will then be confused, and the community doomed.

This selection is the true meaning of the living body.

If you can sincerely examine the words written above and act by them, those surrounding you will rejoice, and those far off will tell your story. And then, why worry about the Way not being carried out or seekers not arriving?"

OBJECTIVITY

"In all cases, when right and wrong are not clear, you must be careful. When right and wrong are clear, you must decide on the basis of reason and common sense, consider where the truth lies, and settle the matter without doubt.

This way, you aren't motivated by dominant arguments and flattery won't confuse you."

HEART-TO-HEART COMMUNICATION

"Tigers and snakes aren't the enemies of vultures and buzzards, but the vultures and buzzards follow them and screech at them. And why? Because they have a cruel heart. Pigs and cows aren't chased by ravens and magpies – these birds gather around and ride on their backs. And why? Because they don't have a cruel heart.

An ancient Chan Master once visited a monk. He found him setting a meal from half-cooked rice. The teacher said, 'Why do crows fly away when they see a man?' The monk was confused; finally he returned the question to the teacher. The teacher said, 'Because I still have a murderous heart.'

And so, those who suspect others are suspected by them, those who forget people are forgotten by people. The ancients, who were friendly with tigers and snakes, understood this principle well. One ancient said, 'An iron bull doesn't fear the roar of a lion – it is just like a scarecrow watching the flowers and birds.' These words take the principle to its completion."

GOVERNMENT

"A rule for governing subjects is that favor should not be extreme, so that the subjects do not become haughty. And authority mustn't be too strict for if it is, the subjects will be resentful.

If you want favor without haughtiness and authority without resentment, give your favors to those with merit, and don't hand them out arbitrarily. Authority should be implemented where there is wrongdoing and shouldn't be used to oppress the weak.

This way, even if your favors are many, people will not become haughty, and although authority is strict they won't be resentful.

On the other hand, if you reward those whose merits aren't worthy of elevation, and severely punish those whose misconducts aren't worth the blame, you will eventually cause people to nurture feelings of haughtiness and resentment."

MEANS

"The way of the enlightened is not without finding the means. Living beyond one's means is a mistake. Not always does your wish come true, so the attempt to fulfill your wishes leads to trouble and confusion.

Many people of the past and present are hasty, careless, and are in danger to the point of reaching destruction.

So then, who can claim that he has no excess? Only wise and talented people use them well; this is praised as excellence."

PEACE IN THE MIDST OF VIOLENCE

"Chan Master Shantang fled to Yunmen hermitage along with the Ministry President Han Zicang, Chan Master Wanan, and one or two other Chan adepts, to avoid the violence of the civil war in the early 1130s.

Mr. Han asked Wanan, 'I heard some time ago that you were captured by the soldiers of the rebel leader Li Cheng. How did you manage to escape?'

Wanan said, 'I was captured and chained, starved and frozen for days till I thought that I would surely die. And then, there was a snowstorm so heavy that it buried the building and caused the walls of the rooms where we were held to collapse. That night, more than a hundred were lucky enough to survive and escape.'

Mr. Han said, 'While captured, how did you cope with your imprisonment?'

Wanan didn't answer. Mr. Han asked him again, pressing him for an answer.

Wanan said, 'Why is it so important that we talk about it? People like us study the Way. We make do with justice for our sustenance and have only death. What is there to fear?'

Mr. Han nodded at this.

From this we know that our predecessors had unchallengeable will-power, even in the midst of mortal calamity and trouble in the world."

Who to Elect

"Chan Master Shantang said when he retired from leadership of the community at Baizhang to the government officer Han Zicang:

'Advanced people from ancient times were virtuous and responsible. That is why they accepted only a third invitation and left with only one farewell.

Among the advanced people of today, only the strong who know when to step forward and when to withdraw without losing the right way, are worthy of being called wise masters.'"

DECENCY

"The attitude of the leader must be fair. When you do things, don't assume that your attitude is necessarily right, while others are wrong. Then, your mind won't fill with likes and dislikes regarding different and same. Then, there will be no way for signs of self-indulgence or worthless prejudices to enter your mind."

EXAMPLES

"The ancients would adopt a good thing when they saw it, and if they made a mistake they would change it. By way of following the path of virtue and developing accord, they hoped to escape without mishaps. They worried about not knowing their own weaknesses, and more than anything, wanted to learn of their mistakes.

Were the ancients like this because their intelligence was unsatisfactory or because their perception wasn't clear? The truth is that this was a warning to those of later times who tried to glorify themselves and belittle others.

The expansion of the community, with people arriving from all over, is not something for only one person to deal with. It is essential to be assisted by the eyes, ears and thoughts of associates in order to fully comprehend what is right, and recognize people's feelings and conditions.

If a person relies on his high station, highly estimates himself, distances himself from minor tasks yet slights the body of the community in general, doesn't know who the wise are, doesn't recognize who isn't good, doesn't change what is wrong, doesn't follow what is right, acts arbitrarily without any deference – this is the basis for catastrophe. How could one not beware?

If it turns out that there aren't any among the associates who are worth consulting, a man must take examples from sages of the past.

If you shut everyone out, you cannot 'let in a hundred rivers to become an ocean.'"

NOMINEES

"While nominating leaders for public study communities, it is essential to nominate those who preserve the Way and are modest and peaceful. Those, when nominated will increase their will and integrity, will not empty the communities' treasury wherever they go, but will fully develop the community and serve as masters of teaching, rescuing the present from decadence.

As for shameless, deceiving scoundrels, people who know how to flatter and cling to authority, those who stick to powerful upper-class families, why should they be nominated?"

COMMON SENSE

"In the whole world, common sense is the only thing that cannot be eliminated. And even if it is oppressed and unexpressed, how can that affect common sense?

That is why, when someone truly enlightened is elected to a spiritual community, all those who see and hear are joyous and praise the choice. If an unsuitable person is elected, people sorrowfully lament the choice.

In reality, it is nothing but common sense. This way, you can figure out whether a Chan community will flourish or decline."

MISREPRESENTATION

"The ancients first chose powerful and enlightened people for the leadership, later they recommended people with ability and learning, to advance at their time.

If one who isn't a good receptacle is placed before others, most of those who see and hear him will slight him, and accordingly, the monks will think to themselves of polishing their reputation and advantages in order to become established.

We have recently seen Chan communities decline because of students who scorn the virtues of the Way and lack integrity and humility. They slander the pure and simple as being crude imbeciles, and praise the shallow and noisy as being smart.

Therefore, it seems that the perceptions of the new leaders aren't clear. They go fishing and hunting in order to exploit and imitate and equip themselves with marks of wisdom and eloquent sayings, getting deeper into it as time goes by, until it has become a decadent trend.

When you talk to them about the Way of the ancient sages, they are as blind as if their eyes are turned to the wall. It is truly impossible to help these people."

MEMORIAL

"In ancient days Huitang wrote in memory of Huanglong, 'those who engaged studies in ancient times, lived among the crags and in caves, ate roots and fruits, wore hides and leaves. They didn't concern themselves with fame and gain, and didn't register their names in government offices.

Since the Wei, Jin, Qi, Liang, Sui, and Tang dynasties (third to ninth centuries C.E.), when sacred places were built for the assemblies of students from all around the country, good people were chosen to lead, so that they would direct the corrupt, and bring the wise to guide the foolish and deluded. Because of that, hosts and guests were established, and superior and inferior were united.

Now when people from all over gather in a sacred place, it truly is difficult to bear the responsibility. It is essential to unify the great and disperse the petty, deal first with the urgent and later with the casual, not plan for oneself but concentrate on helping others.

These words above are as different from selfish ambitions as the sky is from the earth.

Names of many generations of leaders are inscribed in Huanglong's stone sanctuary, so that those who come to see them will look at them and say who was enlightened, who was generous and righteous, who was fair to the whole community, and who rewarded himself.

Can we not beware?"

THE QUALITY OF CANDIDATES

"The position of assembly chief in a Chan community is a rank for which the virtuous and wise are chosen. But these days, in many places, people no longer ask if the leader is good or bad. Everyone uses this position as a stepping-stone for their own ambitions. That is also the mistake of the community teachers. Now, in the age of imitation, it is difficult to find someone for this position.

If you choose those with their actions a bit better than the rest, their virtue a little more complete, who are modest and decent, the result will be somewhat better than choosing those who rush ahead hastily."

DIVISION OF RESPONSIBILITIES

"When the important ancients served as leaders of Chan communities, they didn't manage the community property personally but entrusted it to the care of monastery officials. The abbots of recent times assume extra power and abilities and refer all tasks, big and small, to the abbot while the positions of the officers have been emptied of their content.

If you wish to try and manage all the affairs of the community through the abilities of one person only, keeping people in the picture, informed, just so the general order isn't disturbed, wouldn't that be hard?"

EXILE OF THE MASTER

"When our late teacher Miaoxi began to teach as the leader of Jingshan, he discussed Chan Buddhism in evening gatherings that were held at various places throughout the country. When he came to discuss the teachings of the expiring Cao-Dong school of Chan, he talked on and on. The next day, Assembly Chief Yin, in the past a student of the Cao-Dong school said to him, 'Helping others is a serious matter. A person must want to help activate spiritual teaching; he must save it from fading according to the times – not grasp convenient chances. When you discussed various teachers of the past, when you yourself were a Chan follower, even then it could not have been arbitrary – all the more so now that you are a public teacher.'

The teacher said, 'Last night's discussion was one occasion.'

The assembly chief said, 'The study of saints and sages is based on its nature – how can you slight their honor?'

The teacher bowed his head and apologized, but the assembly chief continued talking about the matter endlessly. Later, when our late teacher Miaoxi was exiled, one of the attendants wrote a statement of his exile and placed it in front of the communal hall. The monks sobbed like people who had just lost their parents, grieving sadly and wandering restlessly.

Assembly Chief Yin approached all the community members and said to them, 'The calamities and stresses of human life are completely inevitable. Had Miaoxi been meek all his life, hiding among people, keeping his mouth closed, not saying anything, this exile surely wouldn't have occurred. But must I remind you that what the sages of the past had to do doesn't stop at this? Why do you insist on torturing yourselves? In ancient times some decent students left together to see the great teacher Fenyang; they ran into military operations taking place in the northeast at the time, so they changed their clothes and mixed in with the troops to make their way up to Fenyang. Now, Miaoxi's place of exile is not so far from here. There are no obstacles or gaps in the road, the mountains and rivers aren't steep and threatening – if you want to see Miaoxi, what is the problem?' After this, the whole crowd became silent. The next day they left in a long and continuous stream."

CRITICISM

"When my late teacher Miaoxi was exiled, there were some students who privately criticized him. Assembly Chief Yin said, 'In general, when criticizing and talking about people, you should try to find where that same fault is flawless – how can you call the flawless faulty? If you don't look into people's hearts, and just doubt their actions, what use is it to the democracy of the community?

Miaoxi's virtue and ability come from nature. In his guidance and his conduct he only follows duty. In thought and reasoning he definitely excels other people. Now that Creation is silencing him, there must be a reason; what can we know other than this might be a blessing for teaching one day?'

Those who heard this no longer criticized."

SAFETY IN THE COMMUNITY

"A man known as a teacher must purify his mind and heart and accept people from all over with the utmost decency. If there is someone among them who embraces the Way and is virtuous, humane and just, you should advance that man, even if resentment exists between you.

And if there is someone who is a twisted misanthrope, you must send that man away, even if you are privately grateful to that man. This way, each person who arrives will know what to expect, so that everyone is of one mind, with the same values. Then the community is safe."

Bringing the Community to Prosperity

"Few leaders can bring a community to prosperity. The reason is that most forget truth and virtue and neglect generosity and duty, abandon the regulations of the Dharma and follow their personal feelings. Considering the decline and disappearance of spiritual schools, a person should be honest but humble towards others, pick out the wise and good for mutual help, respect those with fine, virtuous traits, keep away from petty people, develop himself moderately and frugally and extend virtue to others. After that, those whom you employ as your assistants, hold on to those who are more mature and stay away from the flattering opportunists.

The value of all this is that there will be no slander of corruption and no rift because of disputes."

TROUBLES

"Sages of the past were bothered when they had no troubles, and would say, 'Could God have forgotten the bad?'

A philosopher said, 'Only saints are free from inside and outside troubles. If you aren't a saint, be anxious within when you are at peace.'

Wise and understanding people know that one cannot avoid trouble so they prepare themselves for it from the start. This way, when human life has worry and toil, it may turn into happiness for a whole lifetime.

After all, even the ancient sages – kings of the past – couldn't avoid troubles, calamities, slander and disgrace, all the more so could others."

ROLE-PLAYING

"Recently we see that Chan communities suffer from a shortage of mature people. Everywhere you turn, there are hundreds of people, one serving as a teacher, and the group as his partners. They fool each other when one takes the part of the spiritual monarch, adopting its symbols of office. Even though these frauds give speeches, they have no understanding of the scriptures. That's how it is – there are no mature people.

Until a person purifies his mind and reaches its basis, and acts accordingly, how can he allow himself to teach instead of the Buddha? It would be like someone has been declared emperor by mistake – he brings on himself his death sentence. Spiritual monarchy is even more serious than worldly monarchy – it can't be taken arbitrarily.

The sages of the past are getting more and more distant, while those confined in their imitative schools are multiplying everywhere, causing the teaching of ancient sages to decline with every day that passes. Just as Confucius lamented, 'I would like to stay silent, but can I?'

I stressed here one or two subjects that cripple the Way and desecrate the teachings. I've done it in order to spread these words among the Chan communities, so that the younger generation will know that those who proceeded them worked hard and struggled to plant these great teachings into their minds, like walking on ice or running on swords, not in pursuit of honor or gain.

If those who understand me blame me for it, then I have nothing more to add."

CHAN TEACHERS AND NOBLES

"Lately I've seen nobles, regional inspectors, and governors, enter the mountain monasteries, take care of official business, and the next day send a messenger with word to the chief elder of the monastery, 'Today you must give a special lesson to this or that official.' This situation demands investigation.

Although it is true that such examples have been reported in the books since ancient times, in every case it was the nobleman who came to seek the teacher, while the Chan elder would use the visit to briefly mention the issues of external protection of the teaching and adoration of nature.

When the nobles became followers of the Way, the Chan elders would tell several stories of the school so as to create their respect. There are well-known cases of Confucian nobles seeking and receiving guidance from Chan masters – do you think that this particularly irrational behavior brought on a chuckle from the knowledgeable?"

AUTHORITARIANISM

"When ancient sages meant to hold private meetings, they would first hang a sign outside to announce the meeting, and each individual would arrive prepared because of the greatness of the matter of life and death, eager to settle his doubts and decide what to do.

These days, we often see community leaders inviting everyone, paying their respects in private interviews, even if they are old or ill.

If there is an aroma, it is naturally fragrant – what need is there to announce it? By this, they wrongly create divisions, so hosts and guests feel uncomfortable. Teachers must think of these things."

CHAN HISTORY

"Chan founders bestowed both the teachings and the robe of succession. After six generations, the robe stopped being passed on. Those whose actions and comprehension were suitable were taken to continue the work of the teachings for future generations. The path of Chan became more and more brilliant, with an increasing number of descendants.

After the sixth Chan patriarch, came the two true heirs, the great Masters Shitou and Mazu. The profound words and wonderful sayings of these two great men spread around the country, and from time to time there were some who truly understood their inner meaning.

And when the teachers had many methods, the students had more than one way open.

Even when the original stream of Chan branched out into five different ones, each round or square according to their vessel, the essence of the water remained the same.

Each branch had a superb reputation, and each diligently strived to realize its responsibilities.

That's how Chan communities sprouted up everywhere, not without a reason.

From this time on, the communities would carry out a mutual relationship between one another, revealing the subtleties, deciphering the mysteries, sometimes silently, sometimes publicly, and assisting the process of teaching this way or the other. Their sayings were flavorless, like steamed board soup and rice cooked from nails. These were served to future generations, to chew on.

The practice that evolved from all this is called bringing up the ancients. Poems on ancient tales began with

Fenyang, then with Xuedou. Shortly after, his poems were widely published and he was the one who revealed its essential meaning and boundless extent.

The authors that came later followed Xuedou and imitated him, without including issues of enlightenment and virtue. And yet, they strived for the freshness and brilliance of literary expressions causing future generations of students not to notice the pristine pureness and completeness of the ancients' message.

I have traveled through Chan communities and seen among my predecessors those who read nothing but ancient sayings, and don't practice anything but the original, pure laws of the Chan communities.

Is it because of their special fondness for ancient things?

No, it is simply that people of our time aren't worthy of serving as models. I hope to find people of comprehension and realization to understand me beyond the words."

SEVERAL BAD HABITS

"Recently we see students clinging to prejudiced views, misunderstanding people's conditions, shallow in their faith, rebellious, fond of flatterers, admiring those who follow them and at the same time distancing those who disagree with them.

Even if they have a spark of knowledge or half an understanding, they are still covered by these bad habits. Many of them grow old without reaching achievements."

A FALSE TEACHING

"Everywhere you go in the Chan communities, a false teaching is spreading that says that discipline, meditation and knowledge aren't necessary, and that it is unnecessary to develop virtue or get rid of desires. This kind of talk causes damage not only to current Chan communities; it is actually a destruction of the teachings of ten thousand generations.

Ordinary people have desires, they love and hate and desire, they're selfish and ignorant, and their thoughts are attached to material things, like bubbles in a boiling pot. How can they be cooled and purified? Much of what ancient sages had to think about related to this. So, from here, they set up three subjects of study – discipline, meditation and knowledge – in order to control people, reform and restore them.

Nowadays, young students don't uphold the precepts, don't practice meditation, don't cultivate their knowledge, and don't develop their virtue. They count only on wide learning and powerful intellect; their way of action is plain and crude so it is impossible for them to improve. This is what I meant when I said that such talk leads to the destruction of Chan communities for generations.

Only those lofty-minded people, who travel on steady ground, keeping sincere and faithful to understanding and clarifying the issue of life and death, will not be dragged down by these people. They say that such talk cannot be believed for their talk is like bird droppings, like water drunk by a snake. It is harmful to even read or listen to such talk, all the more so to ingest it, because it will surely kill people. Those who know will naturally stay away from it."

GIFTS OF TEACHING

"It is told that the Chan master Wanan was modest and frugal, and used only extemporal discussions and general debates for contributions. There were monks in the community that criticized him for this.

When Wanan heard this he said, 'To dine on fine food in the morning, and dislike the price of the meal in the evening is for ordinary petty people. Since you focus your thoughts on the importance of life and death, and since you have searched and found an island of peace and solitude, you must think and understand how far you are from accomplishing the practice of the Way, and how far you are from the time of the sages.

How can you be concerned with your greedy desires all the time?'"

CHAN MASTER

"Wanan was humane and considerate. He conducted himself with simplicity and modesty. When he spoke, his words were simple yet full of profound meaning. His studies were wide and his memory strong. He determinedly searched for the reasons for final conclusions, wouldn't stop for a moment, or follow anything in an arbitrary fashion.

When he discussed a story, ancient or current, it was if he had been there personally – to his listeners, things were as clear as if they were seeing them with their own eyes. Students used to say that a year of meditation isn't as good as a day of listening to Wanan's talk."

Buddhism in this Life

"My spiritual grandfather Yuanwu said, 'Few of the Chan people of current times have integrity and loyalty, and there is not one among them who is modest. This is why so many Confucians slight their honor. Someday, you might not be able to avoid acting like this yourself. Therefore, always act according to the rules, don't run after power and gain, and be generous to others.

Life, death, calamity or trouble – let them all happen, and then you will enter the kingdom of Buddhism without leaving the kingdom of demons.'"

A DEMONSTRATION

When Zhong Xiang rebelled in Liyang in 1129, Chan Master Wenshu Dao was in danger. When the power of the rebels grew, his followers fled, but the master said, 'Is it possible to avoid calamity?' and so, by remaining in his room, he was killed by plunderers.

His simple follower Wugou wrote an epilogue to the collection of the master's sayings, 'Loving life and disliking death are normal feeling for human beings. Only perfect human beings acknowledge the fact that they were originally unborn, that their lives are unattached, and they realize that they will never perish. Therefore, even though they are mortals, they have no fear. This is how they cope with times of the distress of death and birth without their determination wavering.

The late teacher was such a person. His enlightened virtues and loyalty to the truth were worthy to teach the communities and set an example for future generations; that is why he was called Zhengdao, True Guide. He was the successor of Chan Master Fojian.'"

CASUAL ATTIRE

"Assembly Chief Bian became teacher and leader of the community at a certain monastery on the holy Mount Lu. He was always "armed" with a bamboo staff and wore straw sandals. When he went to a different monastery, the abbot of that monastery, a monk named Hunrong, scolded him for his appearance, saying, 'A teacher is a model and guide for others; how can you avoid humiliating yourself when you behave like this?'

Bian laughed and said, 'In life, acting as one wishes is considered a pleasure. So why blame me for it?'

He took a paintbrush, wrote a poem, and left.

The poem said:

> *Don't say that I am destitute;*
> *When the body is destitute, the Way isn't.*
> *These straw sandals are as fierce as tigers,*
> *This staff is as dangerous as a dragon.*
> *When thirsty, I will drink the waters of Chan,*
> *When hungry, I eat chestnut thorn balls.*
> *On my mountain, there are people with*
> *Bronze skulls and iron foreheads.*

When the abbot read this he felt ashamed."

SHOW-BOATS

"Statues of dragons can't bring down rain; how can drawings of cakes appease hunger? Monks who have no real virtue and rely on flowery speeches, are like colorfully painted boats that leak – if you place mannequins in them and place them on solid ground, they will look good, but once in the water, facing winds and waves, aren't they in danger?"

PERSONAL RESPONSIBILITY

"The leader, called the elder, teaches in place of the Buddha. This demands self-purification in dealing with the community, extreme honesty and sincerity in executing affairs, and disinclination to divide one's mind while choosing between gain and loss. It is the individual's duty to do so, and so one must definitely act in this way.

Concerning the matter of success or lack of it, even sages of the past couldn't be sure of it – so how can we force it?"

UNIFORMS

"When Fozhi was abbot at Xichan monastery, the monks strived for uniformity. Only Shuian, peaceful and unassuming by nature, took care of his body with utmost simplicity. He stood out in the crowd because of his appearance, and yet never gave it a second thought.

Fozhi scolded him, saying, 'How can you be so unusual?'

Shuian said, 'It isn't that I didn't want the uniform, it is just that I am poor and don't have the means for it. If I had the money, I would like to make a suit or two and join the group. Since I am poor, I can't do anything about it.'

Fozhi chuckled. He knew that Shuian could not be forced, and so he let the matter rest."

THE DISCIPLINE OF AWARENESS

"A racehorse runs quickly, but doesn't dare to gallop freely because of the bit and halter. If petty people don't follow their feelings in a struggle or dispute, it is only because of the rules and punishments. When the flow of consciousness dares not cling to material objects, this is the power of awareness.

If students are unaware and unreflective, they are like a racehorse without a bit and halter, like petty people without laws. With what will they end their greed and passions, and subdue errant thoughts?"

FOUR LIMBS OF LEADERSHIP

"Four limbs has the body of leadership: enlightenment and virtue, speech and action, humaneness and justice, etiquette and law. Enlightenment and virtue are the roots of teaching; humaneness and justice are the branches of teaching. With no roots, it's impossible to stand; with no branches it is impossible to be complete.

Ancient sages noticed that students couldn't control themselves, so they founded Chan communities in order to settle them, and established leadership to guide them. Therefore, the honor of the community is not for the leader, and providing the plentiful necessities of life is not for the students. All of it is for the Way of enlightenment.

Therefore, a good leader must first of all honor enlightenment and good virtues, and be cautious in speech and action. In order to be a student, one must think first of all about goodness and right, and act according to etiquette and law.

Thus, leadership cannot stand without the students, and students can't develop without their leader. Leadership and the students are like the body and arms, like the head and feet. When big and small fit without opposition, they make progress through each other.

And so it is said, 'Students keep the community, communities keep virtue.' If the community has no virtue, the community will be on its way to decline."

THINKING OF TROUBLE

"*The Book of Changes* says, 'An exemplary person sees trouble and prevents it.' Therefore, people of ancient times thought of the great trouble of life and death and prevented it with the Way, until eventually, the greatness of the Way increased and was transmitted for a long time.

Nowadays people think that the vast distances of the search for the Way don't compare to the immediate urgency of material needs. That's why they compete, with their worthless and flashy habits, calculating down to a hair, keeping an eye on everything that passes before them, their hearts full of random schemes.

This way, a person can serve as a guide for current affairs the whole year round, but surely not for issues such as considerations of life and death. This is the reason why students are getting worse from day to day, communities are deteriorating day by day, their uniting principles declining from day to day, until they've reached a point of helplessness from which they can hardly be saved. We must stand aware."

A Direct Shortcut

"Once, when I was traveling in search of the Way, I saw Gaoan at an evening assembly. He said, 'The ultimate Way is a direct shortcut unattached to human sentiments. It is essential that your heart be sincere, and your mind true. Don't be a servant to pretension and partiality. Pretension is near deception, and when you are partial you are imbalanced – none of these two are proper for the ultimate Way.'

I pondered over these words, realized their wisdom and decided to put them into practice. Later, when I saw Fozhi, who was to become my teacher, my mind filled for the first time with great enlightenment. Only then was I able to live up to the ambition of my life pilgrimage."

NIPPING IN THE BUD

"Wherever Yuetang was leader of a Chan community, the task of the Way became his own personal responsibility. He didn't send out fund-raisers, neither did he visit nobles. He used only what the monastery provided him for the livelihood of his people. He refused many monks who asked to gather alms.

Some said, 'The Buddha ordered the poor to take their food bowls and beg for a living; how can you stop them and not permit it?'

Yuetang said, 'This was all right in the Buddha's day, but I'm afraid that if we permit this today, those who pursue gain will end up enslaving themselves.'

I believe that Yuetang's nipping in the bud was sharp, cutting and entirely clear. His practical words still echo in my ears. When I observe the current situation through that point of view, haven't things gone even further than people enslaving and selling themselves?"

MERIT CERTIFICATE

"Once the astronomer Huang Luzhi said, 'Chan Master Huanglong Huinan was profound in mind, generous in considerations, and uninfluenced by any other thing. All his life, he had no pretensions. Among his followers there were those who never saw him happy or angry. He treated everyone with equal decency, even the servants and workers. Therefore, he was able to bring the Way of Ciming to flourish without raising his voice or changing his expression. It wasn't without a reason."

A THOUSAND DAYS OF EFFORT

"When the ancient nobles were leaders, they were involved in carrying out the Way, never neglecting or rebelling, not even for a minute. Those days, the great Chan master Fenyang, used to lament how flawed the era of imitation was, how complicated it was to teach the students; but his excellent student Ciming said, 'It is all very simple- the trouble is that the teaching masters don't guide very well, that's all.'

Fenyang said, 'The ancients were pure and honest, and it still took them twenty to thirty years to reach achievement.'

Ciming said, 'These are not the words of a sage. For a person proceeding along the Path in a correct fashion, it is a matter of a thousand days of effort.' Some didn't listen and claimed that Ciming was speaking nonsense.

The region where Fenyang worked was very cold so he decided to stop the customary evening gathering. A foreign monk said to Fenyang (one version of the story is that an Indian monk came to him in a dream), 'There are six great heroes in this assembly, why don't you teach?' And before three years had passed, there were actually six people in Fenyang's group who realized enlightenment."

EXCHANGE TRADE

"Lately we bump into leaders in various places who try to control their followers with mind tricks, while their followers serve their leaders with ulterior motives of influence, power, and gain.

In fact, the leaders and their followers are dealing in exchange trade, above and below are fooling each other. How can education and communities flourish?"

MOVING PEOPLE

"Shuian advised a follower who was invited to testify in court:

'In order to move people through words, one must be true and sincere. If your words aren't true and to the point, the reaction that they will induce will be shallow – and then who will take them seriously?

In ancient times, our spiritual father Baiyun, sent his student, our great spiritual grandfather Wuzu, to a teaching assignment, warning him in these terms:

'The Chan Way is in decline and in danger, like eggs piled up. Don't sink into neglect and irresponsibility. This uselessness kills time and upsets the ultimate virtue. You must act peacefully and with an open mind, estimate proper measures. Help people, think of the whole community. Bring out the truth and that way pay back your debt to the enlightened ones and ancient spiritual fathers.'

Who would not be moved hearing those words?

Lately you have been invited to speak before the imperial court. That is truly promising for the teaching. In honor of the Way, you must be humble. Don't let your pride hurt you.

Since ancient times, sages have been modest and gentle, respectful and reasonable. They held themselves with complete virtue and didn't praise authority or rank. This way, they were able to purify a whole era, their fame resounding beautifully for ten thousand generations.

I think that my days are few, and that we will never again meet in person. This is the reason for this urgent caution.'"

Retirement

"Since youth, Shuian was extraordinary, with great determination. He appreciated decency and character, stayed away from foolish waste, didn't pursue petty words of criticism. He had an open heart and mind. He acted according to principles. He never seemed depressed even if he was plagued by calamity and trouble.

Shuian was abbot for eight public monasteries, in four different cities. Everywhere he went, he worked hard to establish the practice of the Way at heart.

In 1178 he retired from the Pure Kindness monastery on West Lake. He wrote:

Six years of sweeping and cleaning temples in the imperial capital;

Tiles and pebbles turn to celestial rooms.

Today the palace is standing firm, and I return;

A pure wind rises from all directions from the staff.

The nobles and commons tried to convince him to stay there but to no avail. He sailed in a small boat up the river to Heavenly Brightness monastery in the Longwater region.

Shortly after, he fell ill, left the assembly and announced his end."

THE NEGLECTED GENERATION

"In ancient times, Chan Master Baizhang, from Great Wisdom monastery, was concerned by the laziness and haughtiness of the monks of the neglected generation. He drew up special rules and guidelines in order to prevent this. Each monk was given responsibility according to his talents and abilities.

The leader lived in a ten-foot-square room, and the community lived in a common hall, strictly managed, with ten assembly chiefs. Their lives were managed like a civil government: the leaders brought up the essentials of teachings; the subjects took care of the facets of it. This caused the above and below to understand each other just like a body using its arms, the arms using its fingers – each obeyed.

Therefore, since the legacy of the ancients hadn't disappeared completely, our predecessors who followed the tradition and received help from it and practiced it carefully could do so because of their remaining influence.

Lately we see Chan communities decline and change. Students appreciate talent and slight industriousness of practice; they are fond of the grandiose and casual and slight the truth and simplicity. With time, they get themselves into a decedent trend.

Decadence first begins with taking things easy, but after this lengthy indulgence and habituation, it becomes second nature and people don't treat it as a mistake or something contrary to principle.

These days, the leader timidly fears the subordinates, while they, in turn, keep a wary eye on their superiors.

When the leader is relaxed, his subordinates speak sweetly and grovel for his favors, but when they find an opening they treacherously scheme how to bring him down. Those who win are considered wise, while those who fail are considered foolish – no longer questioning the order of nobility and the unkindness, or the principles of justice and injustice. An act exercised by one, will be imitated by the other; those above will obey those below, what's done before, will continue after.

Unless clever teachers gather their power of will and pile up a hundred years of effective work, this debauchery and stagnation cannot be changed."

WATERING MELONS AT MIDDAY

"Yuetang's longest leadership was at the Pure Kindness monastery. Someone told him, 'You have practiced the Way here for years, yet I've never heard of any successors among your followers. Aren't you shaming your teacher?'

Yuetang didn't answer.

That same man repeated his question one day and Yuetang said, 'Haven't you heard the story of the man in ancient times who planted melons? He was very fond of them and watered them at midday in the middle of summer. As a result, they rotted in the fields. So what does that mean? Not that his fondness for melons wasn't earnest, but that his watering wasn't on time, and by that he ruined them.

Old teachers in different places support monks without observing whether their work with the Way is fulfilled in them, or if their capacity is wide and extensive. All they want is to hurry their success. But when you carefully examine their morals, they are corrupt, and when you examine their words and observe their actions, you find them contradictory. What they call correct and impartial is harmful and prejudiced.

Isn't there an issue of fondness that exceeds its limits? This is just like watering melons at midday. As for myself, I fear that I will be a laughingstock in the eyes of the knowing so I don't do it.'"

No Fixed Classes

"The great spiritual Way is clear and open. Noone on the Way was originally wise or foolish. It is like a case of certain ancients who started their way plowing and fishing but became advisors to emperors – how could that happen if there were fixed classes of intelligence?

Anyway, it requires certain personal power to take a part in this."

DIAGNOSES

"Many monks develop illnesses because of Chan. Those with sick ears and eyes think that staring and glaring, inclining the ear and nodding, are Chan tasks. Those with sick tongues and mouths think that Chan tasks are expressed in crazy talk and wild shouts. Those with sick hands and feet think that Chan means walking back and forth, waving the hands east and west. Those with sick hearts and guts think that exploring the mysterious, learning the marvelous, transcending feelings and detaching oneself from the views is Chan.

Speaking from a practical point of view, all the conditions described are sicknesses.

Only a true teacher can clearly discern the subtle signs, know at a glance if people understand or not, discern whether they know or not the minute they've opened the door. Later, while using a needle and awl, the teacher frees them from hidden traps, presses their weak spots, examine if they're genuine or fake – all this without adhering to only one method, and aware as to when to consider and change – to cause them to eventually walk into the kingdom of peace, happiness and freedom from concerns, even before the teacher finally finishes his work."

LEADERSHIP PRACTICE

"In order to train yourself to deal with the assembly, it is necessary to use wisdom. First of all, you must be aware in order to disperse illusions and distance sentimentality.

If you turn away from awareness and mix with the dusts, your mind will be hazy. When one doesn't distinguish between wisdom and foolishness, things get complicated."

THE BLUE CLIFF RECORD

"The Way that is especially passed on outside of doctrine is essentially simple and exemplary. From the beginning there is no other discussion but this; our predecessors carried it out with no doubt and without deviation.

During the Tianxi era of the Song dynasty (1012-1022), Chan master Xuedou, wrote poems on the ancient stories using his verbal skills, his eloquence, and beautiful ideas in diversified display, seeking freshness and sharpening his skill. He followed the example of Fenyang and hoped to catch and control the students of the time.

From this point on, the manner of Chan changed.

Later on, during the Xuanho era (1119-1125), Yuanwu also published his ideas on Xuedou's verses and stories. From then on, the collection was known as The Blue Cliff Record. The perfect masters of the time – Wayfarer Ning, Huanglong, Sixin, Lingyuan, and Fojian, couldn't contradict his words, so new students of the later generations prized his words. They recited them by day and memorized them by night, calling it the highest study. No one realized that this was a mistake, and unfortunately the students' meditational abilities deteriorated.

In the beginning of the Shaoxing era (1131-1163), Yuanwu's enlightened successor Miaoxi, went to eastern China and saw that Chan students there were unruly, studying this book to such an extent that it took them to bad places. So he broke the wooden blocks of *The Blue Cliff Record* and analyzed its explanations in order to get rid of delusions and save the confused and floundering, strip away the excess and clear away the exaggerations, demolish the false and revive the true, dealing with the text in a special way.

Gradually, the students realized their mistake and no longer idolized the book.

And so, if not for Miaoxi's high illumination and far sight, the Chan communities would be in peril."

BREAKING THROUGH OBSTRUCTION
BY REASON

"When Fojian was leader of the Great Peace community, Gaoan was in charge of taking care of the guests. He was young and lively and looked down on everyone else. Only few gained his approval.

One day, during lunch when Gaoan rang the bell, he saw one of the workers placing food before Fojian in a special bowl. He left the hall announcing in a loud voice, 'If the teacher of five hundred monks acts like this, how can he serve as an example for later students?'

Fojian pretended not to see or hear a thing.

Later, when Fojian left the room, Gaoan checked his bowl and found that it contained pickled vegetables. It turned out that Fojian had a chronic stomach ailment and that he didn't touch oil, which was used daily in the food of the monastery.

Gaoan was ashamed and left for the leader's room to announce his resignation.

Fojian said, 'What you said was quite right. But it just happens that I am sick, that's all. I heard that an ancient sage said, 'Break through all obstructions by reason.' Since what I eat is not better, the community does not doubt me.

Your temperament and will-power are clear and far-reaching; the day will come when you will be a cornerstone of the source teaching. Don't let this incident stick in your mind.'

When Fojian moved on to another monastery, Gaoan left and later became his successor."

TEACHING GOVERNMENT OFFICIALS

"When discoursing on the Way with government officials, during the dialogue you must peel from them their intellectual comprehension, and disable them from clinging to clichés. It is simply necessary to purely clarify their single attempt to rise above.

The late teacher Miaoxi once said, 'When you meet nobles, answer their questions only. Avoid any other subject.'

A person hearing these words must be such a person as well in order to be of help to the times and keep the living Buddhism from harm."

THE PERIL OF LEADERSHIP

"A good country nurtures its beings, a generous leader nurtures his people properly. Nowadays, many who are considered leaders don't take their people seriously and prefer taking care of their own needs. They don't enjoy hearing good words, they like covering up their own mistakes when they indulge in improper habits and spend time vainly pleasing themselves.

When petty people give in to the likes and dislikes of the leaders, isn't the path of leadership in danger?"

KILLED BUT NOT SHAMED

"The Lay Master of Purple Cliff said, 'My former teacher Miaoxi puts integrity, justice and courage as his first priorities in daily life. He can be befriended but not estranged, approached but not estranged, killed but not shamed.

His dwelling is humble and his food simple. He deals with the problems and troubles of life and death as if they are nothing. He is an example to what was meant by the saying 'It is hard to clash with the sword of the great blacksmith.' His only concern is an unpredicted injury.' Eventually, things turned out just as the laymen said."

CHOOSING ASSISTANTS

"As a leader, Ye-an understands the processes of the human mind and is aware of the community's great body. Once he told me, 'In order to be host in a place, you must choose active and decisive people for assistants. They are like a comb for the hair, or a mirror for a face – then what is beneficial and what is harmful, what is proper and what is improper, all these can't be hidden.'"

Depth and Shallowness

"Students of the current age are shallow, they overestimate their ears and underestimate their eyes, and eventually, not one of them can plunge into the depth of mystery.

And so, let us say, 'No matter how high the mountain is, craggy cliffs and bamboo bushes are at its pinnacle; no matter how deep the sea, currents and whirlpools are in its depths.'

If you want to study the Great Way, the essence of the matter is in the investigation of its depths and peaks. After that you can throw light on the complex mysteries and adapt accordingly, without limits."

THE MINDS OF SAINTS AND SAGES

"The minds of saints and sages are tolerant and easygoing, and yet, their minds are clear. They're cool and relaxed, but their actions are recognizable.

They are patient concerning the outcomes of their actions, and always ready to keep on with them for a lengthy period. They aren't willing to insist on advancement, but approve of making the effort in order to achieve the Way.

Those who understand the will of the saints and sages from these words, and maintain it for over a thousand generations, will be like this."

REVIEWING HISTORY

"Before Bodhidharma, the founder of Chan, there wasn't such a thing as Chan monasticism, the institutionalization of the living wonder of Buddhism.

The offsprings of Bodhidharma, who carried out the Way as an answer to the world, were pressured and couldn't prevent this development – but they still lived in simple huts that sheltered them from the wind and rain, and ate little if only to appease their hunger. They were gaunt and haggard as a result of hardships; some of them could no longer stand their suffering, and the kings and nobles who wanted to see them, could not.

That is why everything they created was free and unfettered, shaking the heavens and moving the earth.

In later generations, they stopped being like this. Hidden in their towers, with rich food and clothing, they had whatever they wanted. At this point, forces of evil started to affect their minds; they clung to the gates of temporal leaders wagging their tails and begging for pity, in extreme cases deceiving and usurping by status, like stealing gold in broad daylight – completely ignoring that there is such thing in the world as cause and outcome.

The letters of Chan Master Miaoxi expose the current mental habits of each and every one and do not leave out even a crumb, like the legendary pond water that enables you to see what occurs within it clearly. If you can receive them with faith and put them into practice, what's the need to specially seek Buddhism besides?"

THE REVIVAL OF THE LINJI SCHOOL OF CHAN

"In ancient times, Miaoxi revived the Way of Linji in the autumn of its decline and reduction; but according to his nature, he esteemed humility and emptiness. He never flaunted or published his motives or considerations, never in his life did he turn to people of power and authority, and neither did he grab profit or support.

Miaoxi once said, 'Many matters cannot be accomplished by taking the easy way, or existing on a haughty position. It seems that there are things that are beneficial to the times and helpful to the people, things that originate in error and are worthless. If you indulge in the latter and haughtily take it easy, you are bound to fail.' I took his words to heart and they were a lesson in life for me."

HABIT

"The rise and decline of Chan communities is in their management and principles. Refining students or corrupting them lies in their customs and habits. Even if the ancients lived in caves and nests, living off fruit trees and streams, to live like this now would be unsuitable. Even if people of the present dress and eat richly, to live like this in ancient times would have been unsuitable. Isn't it all just a matter of habits?

What people view as ordinary, they inevitably assume should be all over the world. If they are urged to give this opinion up and quickly adopt a different one, not only will they doubt and disbelieve, they probably won't agree.

When things are considered in this light, it is made clear that people feel secure in their habits, and fear things they have never experienced before. This is their ordinary condition, so why should we wonder about it?"

The Good and the Corrupt

"My late teacher Yengan used to say, 'The good and the corrupt are opposites and all we have to do is distinguish between them. The good maintain truth, kindness, generosity and justice. The corrupt are devoted to power and profit, and act by flattery and deceit. The good accomplish their will and will always do what they learned. The corrupt in high ranks are mostly addicted to their own selfishness, envious of the wise and able; they follow their desires and pursue material possessions; there is no telling how far they're willing to go.

That is why, when there are good people in the community, the community flourishes, and when the community employs corrupt people it declines.

Even if there is one corrupt person among them, it is surely impossible for there to be peace and harmony.'"

THREE DON'TS

"In leadership there are three don'ts: when there is too much work to do, don't be afraid; when there is nothing to do, don't be hasty; don't talk about opinions of right and wrong.

A successful leader who excels in these three things won't be confused or deluded by external objects."

Wolves in Sheepskins

"When there are simple people in a community whose everyday behavior is bad, and have a known history of being bad people, there is no reason for worry; but if those who aren't good within are called sages by the community, then that is truly worrisome."

THE MIRROR REVEALS THE TRUTH

"When you are being slandered, you must accept it docilely. One shouldn't hear the words of others and arbitrarily determine narrow views.

Mostly, flattering opportunists come in groups. Twisted cleverness has many methods: those with prejudice in their hearts like to broadcast their private wishes; those who nurture jealousy unambiguously negate public discussions and consensus.

All in all, these people have narrow and restricted goals, their vision is short-sighted and dim; they think that the different are necessarily unique, and those who undermine open discussions are exceptional.

However, as long as you know that your actions are ultimately right, and that their slander is truly against themselves things will become clear with time; you mustn't refer to things specially, you don't have to insist on your rightness and insult people."

MAKING CHOICES

"Generally, when people are sincere and headed in the right direction, they can still be activated, even if they are slow witted. If they are flatterers with ulterior motives, they eventually cause harm, even if they are clever.

Usually, if people's mental inclination is wrong, they don't deserve to be stationed in positions of service and leadership – even if they are talented and able."

Making Distinctions

"Before a precious stone is cut, it is just a stone; before a racing horse competes, he is mixed with the rest of the animals. When cut and polished, raced and tested, the precious stone is distinguished from the fieldstone, and the racing horse from a wheel horse.

Among the crowd are beggars of virtue and wisdom who have not yet been employed. How can they be distinguished?

It is essential that highly perceptive people be elected by public consensus of the crowd, entrusted on matters of office, tested for their talent and ability, judged by their achievements. Thus, they will prove the great distance between themselves and the average."

LOSS OF ORDER

"The Chan Master of Great Wisdom Baizhang Huihai (720-814) especially established a pure set of rules to help save the poor people of the community from the corruption into which they had fallen in the age of spiritual decline. Since then, sages have followed and applied those rules meticulously. There was teaching, there was order, and there was consistency.

At the end of the Shaoxing era (1160), there were still mature people in the communities who preserved the traditional laws and did not permit themselves to ever deviate from them. In recent years they have lost the order of the schools, and the set of rules is corrupt or confused. Therefore it is said, 'Remove one curtain and many eyes will see the light; neglect one opportunity and many affairs will collapse.' The situation has just reached the point where order no longer works, and communities have stopped flourishing.

But the ancients personified the basic principle, whereby making the growth straight. They preferred making do with the concern of preserving the measures of teaching, rather than worry that the students won't reach their goals.

What they considered right was honest and decent. Leaders in various places nowadays mix decency with indecency, and use the leafage to guide the roots. Those above prefer profit on practicing the Way, while those below covet wealth without fulfilling their duties.

When those above and those below are confused and disorganized, hosts and guests are mixed up, how can we turn the wearers of the patchwork robes towards the truth, and have the communities flourish?"

SELECTION OF BUDDHAS

"Master Huoan Ti first studied with Si-an Yuan Budai at Huguo monastery on top of the famous and holy mountain Tiantai. During a lecture in the teaching hall, Si-an quoted the poem of Laymen Feng on "Selection of Buddhas". When he came to the line 'This is the place for selecting Buddhas,' Si-an shouted. At that moment Houan was greatly enlightened.

He composed a verse on his realization:
Where the assessment ends, the subject is revealed.
At the end of the road, you enter an examination place.
Here is a small hint – rain and wind are swift.
There is no graduation party this time.

After this, he secluded himself on Mount Tiantai. The deputy head of state, Mr. Qian, admired his character and insisted that he respond to the needs of the world by serving as a public teacher at a certain monastery. When Huoan heard of this he said, 'I can't hang out a lamb and sell dog meat,' and disappeared into the night."

RECOGNITION

"At the beginning of the Jiandao era (1165-1174) when Xiatang was the resident master of a public monastery, he saw Huoan's tribute on a portrait of Yuantong:

Not resting on the fundamental, he disturbs our peace
Looking up at him as if blind.
The scenery of Capital City extends through time –
Who is that walking, groping along the wall?

Xiatang was startled and excited. He said, 'I didn't realize that Si-an had such successors.' Then he searched for Huoan everywhere until he found him in Jiangxin. He invited him from among the crowd to fill the position of first in the assembly."

FULFILLMENT OF CONDITIONS

"At the beginning of the Jiandao era, Huoan wandered over to Tiger Hill to see Xiatang. Men of monasteries and common folk of the capital there had heard of his noble manners and tried to nominate him to be the resident teacher at Jiaobao temple in the city.

When Huoan heard of this he said, 'My late teacher Si-an has instructed me, 'Another day, meeting old age, stay.' It seems that this condition has been fulfilled.'

And so, he gladly accepted the invitation to stay there. It turned out that the ancient name of Jiaobao temple was Laoshouan, Old Age Hermitage."

An Improvised Talk

"After Huoan entered Jiaobao temple, one of the patrons asked him to give an improvised talk. He said, 'The Great Spiritual Way is constant and unchangeable; material things deteriorate and must change. In ancient times, the great Chan masters took lessons from the study of antiquity, considered what was appropriate and what wasn't, holding the middle way, working to unify the hearts and minds of people, with enlightenment as the guide. This is why their simple manner, cold as ice, hasn't disappeared until this very day. But in terms of the Chan school, even maintaining comprehension before anything is said harms the manner of our religion, and even discerning clearly on the moment of hearing a phrase buries the enlightened ones.

Even though it is so, 'Going, I reach the water's end; sitting, I watch when the clouds enter.'

Thenceforth, monks, nuns and common folk rejoiced in things they had never heard before, and a whole city of people rested under his wing."

CONTROLLING WILD FOXES

"Once, when Huoan was teaching publicly, nobles and common folk streamed in to take refuge with him. One of the beggars brought the rumor to Tiger Hill, and Xiatang said, 'That mountain ruffian is using blind man's Chan to control a bunch of wild fox ghosts.'

When Huoan heard of this, he replied with a poem
> *You may not like mountain ruffians,*
> *Who lead a group and effortlessly maintain order,*
> *Rising above convention, waving a broom upside down,*
> *Blind man's Chan controlling the wild fox monks.*

Xiatang just laughed."

BALANCE

"Huoan said to Minister of State Ceng Tai: 'The important point in studying the Way is like balancing stones while weighing things: just get them even, that's all. It won't work if one side is heavier.

Pushing ahead and lagging behind are both alike in their one-sidedness. When you understand this, you can learn the Way.'"

TALENT AND CAPACITY

"People's talent and capacity are naturally big or small, since they cannot be taught.

Those with a small piece of paper cannot wrap large objects; those with a short piece of rope cannot pull themselves out of a deep well. An owl can catch a parasite and see a hair at night, but when the sun comes up, it hurts the owl's eyes so that he can't even see a hill.

It seems that the distribution is decided from the start."

A MOMENT IN HISTORY

"Chan Master Jiantang Ji lived on Mount Guan in Fanyang for twenty years, making soup from herbs and millet for his meals; he had purified his mind from fame and success.

Once, as he came down the mountain he heard the sound of weeping by the side of the road. Feeling pity, he went to check the matter. It turned out that there was a whole family, all of them cold and sick. Two of the family members had just died, and they were so poor that they had nothing to put the bodies in. Jiantang went especially into town to buy the coffins to bury them. Everyone who heard of this in the village was touched.

The minister, Mr. Li, said to the nobles, 'Old Ji of our area is a poor man whose heart if filled with the Way; he bestows kindness as well as material goods. How can we let him stay forever on Mount Guan?'

Military Inspector Wang, who at the time was patrolling along the various main roads, reported this in Jiujiang, and the district governor, Mr. Lin Shuda, had the teaching position in Yuantong vacated and invited Jiantang there. When Jiantang heard this request he said, "My Way has become practiceable.' He gladly took his staff and went there.

In order to explain his teaching he said, 'Yuangtong doesn't open a fresh herb shop – I just sell everyone a dead cat's head. I don't know who doesn't think or believe – upon partaking the body will cover with cold sweat.'

The people of the monastery and the common folk were shocked and thought this was unusual. Later, this teaching center flourished greatly."

SHARING

"When people of ancient times improved themselves and controlled their minds, they shared the Way with others. When they undertook tasks and completed their work, they shared their achievements with others. When the Way was accomplished and achievement revealed, they shared their fame with others. This is why everything in the Way was clear; every achievement was completed, all the fame was glorious.

People nowadays are not like that. They are entirely concerned with their own ways, and only worry that someone might surpass them. They don't pursue good and working for what is right, because they glorify themselves. While concentrating on personal achievements, they don't want others to share it with them.

Also, they don't trust the wise and don't get along with the talented, they being too busy praising themselves. Their sole concern is their personal fame, without sharing it with others. They cannot guide people with humility, because they consider themselves successful.

That is why the Path cannot prevent obscurity, their achievements cannot prevent loss, their fame cannot prevent dishonor. This is the great distinction between students of ancient and modern times."

GROWTH

"Studying the Way is like planting a tree – if you cut it just as it begins to branch out, the tree can be used for firewood; if you cut it when it has reached its full growth, its wood can be used for roof beams; if you cut the tree when it is stronger, they can be used for house beams; and if you cut the tree when it is old and huge, you will have pillars.

Isn't it possible that if you postpone achievement to the far future, your profit will be greater?

That is why ancient people saw to it that their Way be sure and great and not narrow, that their will and determination be far-reaching and profound, and their words lofty and kind.

Although they dealt with the contradictions of times, experienced extreme conditions such as hunger and cold, perishing in the mountains and valleys, the strength left in their legacy bridged over hundreds and thousands of years, and people of later times still pass it on as religious law.

Had the ancients been narrow in their Way, had they let in random people, had they searched for satisfaction of immediate ambitions, talking mindlessly, serving authority – their profit would have ended with short-lived fame. How could there have been improvement left over for the future generations?"

A Successor to the Ancients

"The ancients calmed their minds and erased their self-consciousness in mountains and valleys. They drank from streams and ate from trees, in the manner of those who have no thought of gain and success. And yet, there came a time when they were called before the emperors.

The ancients hid their light and concealed their tracks in the mills and various menial chores. In the beginning they had no thoughts of fame or achievement, and finally, they held positions of torch-bearers.

Therefore, the Path, when reached unintentionally, is great, and the virtue universal. Fame, when sought with ambition, is narrow and low.

But your measures and capacities are steady and far-reaching, and worthy of following the ancients. That is why you managed living on Mount Guan for seventeen years and finally became a fine vessel of truth in the community.

Monks today have nothing to concentrate on within, while outwardly pursuing foolish frills which distract them. They have little foresight, and no sense of the general community. As a result, they cannot help with spiritual teaching, and so, are far away from you."

The Normal Condition of Human Beings

"The normal condition of human beings is that only few are free from delusions. Usually, they are immersed in their beliefs, obstructed by their doubts, weakened by their mockery, flooded by their desires.

Once belief is biased, when people hear words they don't think of the truth, until they reach words that exceed what is right. When doubts are extreme, people no longer listen to words even if they are true, and wake up only when they hear lies.

When people don't respect others, they lose the ability to see the good in them. When people are swept away by feelings of love, they'll stay around those who they should keep away from. All these are indulgences in private feelings without considering logic, eventually forgetting the Way of enlightened ones and losing the heart of the community.

Sages take seriously feelings that ordinary people don't. An ancient worthy said, 'Those who plan far ahead first check what is in reach. Those who strive for the great must be careful of the small.'

This should be a matter of a wide range of possibilities and the responsible use of them; surely this isn't a matter of worshipping the high and liking the unusual."

A Chan Master

"Jiantang was of a pure and clear mind. He reached people with kindness and generosity. If students made small mistakes, he would cover for them and protect them in order to develop their merits. He once said of this, 'Who doesn't make mistakes? Excellence is a matter of correction.'

When Jiantong lived on Mount Guan in Fanyang, once in the middle of winter it rained and snowed continuously for so long that he ran out of food. And yet, the teacher behaved as if he weren't aware of the matter. On this occasion, he wrote a poem:

The fire is out, the knapsack empty,
The snow is like apricot blossom
　　　　　falling at the end of the year.
On my head a patchwork robe,
　　　　　burning scraps of wood,
I am peaceful, unaware of my body.
In daily life I walk on the Way, by myself,
Not rushing after honor and fame.

The day he answered the request to be teacher of Yuantong monastery on holy Mount Lu, he came with only a staff in his hand and straw sandals on his feet. Those who saw him looked refreshed and felt relieved. The governor of the Nine Rivers region, Mr. Lin Shuda, said when he saw him, 'This is the bridge to Buddhism.'

From this day on, his name was honored everywhere. His behavior truly matched the nature of the ancient masters. On the day he died, even the servants and workers of the monastery cried."